Baseball

Baseball

Mike Kennedy

Watts LIBRARY™

Franklin Watts
A Division of Scholastic Inc.
New York • Toronto • London • Auckland • Sydney
Mexico City • New Delhi • Hong Kong
Danbury, Connecticut

Note to readers: Definitions for words in **bold** can be found in the Glossary at the back of this book.

Photographs © 2003: AP/Wide World Photos: 19 (Leon Algee), 25 (Roberto Borea), 26 (Ron Frehm), cover (Chris Gardner), 32 (Frank Gunn), 41 (John Hayes), 35 (Lenny Ignelzi), 5 left, 24 (David Kohl), 43 (Bill Kostroun), 36 (Erik S. Lesser), 22 (Pat Little), 17 top (John Rooney), 2 (Justin Sullivan), 30 (John Todd), 33 (Nick Wass), 11, 14, 17 bottom, 20, 44, 47 bottom, 49; Corbis Images: 18 (Bettmann), 27 (Reuters NewMedia Inc.); National Baseball Library: 5 right, 8, 10, 13, 47 top; Negro Leagues Baseball Museum, Inc.: 15; Team Stewart, Inc.: 38; The Image Works: 51 (Rachel Epstein), 29 (Jeff Greenberg), 6, 12, 28 (Peter Hvizdak); Transcendent Algraphics: 9.

The photograph opposite the title page shows Barry Bonds jogging around the bases after the 612th home run of his career.

Library of Congress Cataloging-in-Publication Data

Kennedy, Mike.
    Baseball / by Mike Kennedy.
       p. cm.—(Watts library)
    Summary: Discusses the sport of baseball including its history, rules and regulations, statistics, and some outstanding players.
    Includes bibliographical references and index.
    ISBN 0-531-12271-9 (lib. bdg.)   0-531-15588-9 (pbk.)
    1. Baseball—Juvenile literature. [1. Baseball.] I. Title. II. Series.
GV867.5.K46 2003
796.357—dc21

2003000124

Contents

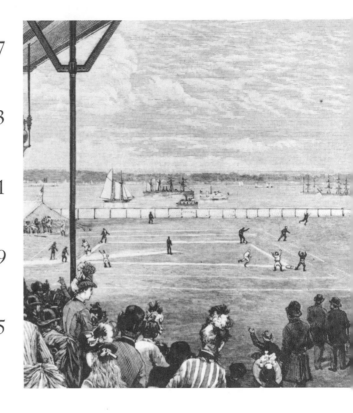

Baseball has changed a great deal since its birth in the 1800s, but it remains a favorite of children and teenagers.

Chapter One

Talkin' Baseball

Of all the team sports that originated in America, baseball is the oldest. It has been called the "grand old game" and the country's national **pastime.** But ironically the sport began as a "grown-up" version of several kids' games and was first played only in small pockets of the northeastern United States. This may make you wonder: How did baseball become so popular and capture the nation's imagination so completely? The story starts almost two hundred years ago.

Join the Club

In the early 19th century, American men in their twenties and thirties in search of new friends joined social clubs. There they discussed current events and celebrated special occasions. When the weather cooperated, they ventured outside to play bat and ball games, such as the English sports of cricket and rounders. A lingering dislike for all things British (left over from the American Revolution and the War of 1812) led them to seek a new sport that they could call their own.

This sketch shows fans enjoying an early version of baseball in Staten Island, just miles from the sport's birthplace.

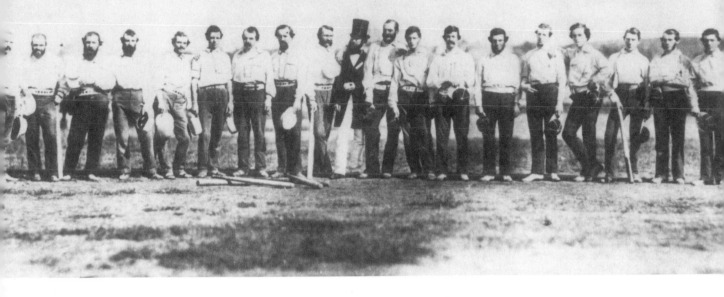

Games called "Base Ball" were played as early as the 1820s. In 1845, a man from New York City named Alexander Joy Cartwright Jr. designed the modern baseball field, founded the Knickerbocker Base Ball Club and devised the sport's initial set of rules. The Knickerbockers played the first official game a year later across the Hudson River at Elysian Fields in Hoboken, New Jersey. Baseball then was somewhat different from today's version. Pitchers threw underhand and stood just 45 feet (14 meters) from home plate. Some hitters used bats that were flat on one side, and they ran toward the ball as they swung. Gloves had not yet been invented. The ball was softer, however, so fielding and catching it did not hurt as much as it might seem.

Baseball was played primarily in northern states such as New York and New Jersey and throughout New England until the 1860s. During the Civil War, Union soldiers from the Midwest learned the game in army camps, and

The New York Knickerbockers and the Brooklyn Excelsiors in 1858, before taking the field for a game.

Northerners captured in battle taught the sport to Southerners. After the war, baseball spread to the West with prospectors and pioneers.

Organized Ball

As baseball's popularity rose, competition on the field intensified. Newspapers began running detailed reports of games. Players improved their skills and invented clever new strategies. Rules were changed almost every year to keep up with these advancements, but changes didn't always happen overnight. For example, it took almost twenty-five years before baseball settled on three strikes as an out and four balls as a walk.

In 1869, the Cincinnati Red Stockings caused a sensation when they traveled east and defeated the best teams in the country. Although ball clubs had been paying their best players for many years, Cincinnati was the first team made up entirely of professionals. Two years later the first pro league, known as the National Association of Professional Base Ball Players, was established.

During this time, professional games attracted large, **raucous** crowds. On the

With their national tour in 1869, the Cincinnati Red Stockings helped lay the groundwork for the first professional baseball league.

field, players sometimes got just as rowdy. Team owners realized how much money they would make if they could gain better control of the sport. A businessman named William Hulbert suggested that the owners work together. In 1876, he founded the National League (NL). According to most historians, this was the beginning of "Major League Baseball."

A few years later, in 1879, Boston Red Caps co-owner Arthur Soden devised the reserve clause, which stripped players of their right to play for any team they wanted. Owners now reserved the rights to their players—either they played for their team, or they did not play at all. Needless to say, the NL owners were **ruthless** and **shrewd** in all their business dealings. This helped them survive challenges from three upstart leagues during the 1880s and 1890s.

As the 20th century dawned, the National League finally met its match. The American League (AL) established teams in some of the country's fastest-growing cities, and went head-

The American League squad posed for this picture in 1933 at the first All-Star Game. They beat the National League, 4-2.

As the World Turns

When the NL agreed to accept the AL as a second major league in 1903, the owners of the pennant-winning Pittsburgh and Boston clubs decided to revive the World Series, an exhibition that had first been played in the 1880s. The new World Series proved so popular it was made the game's official championship in 1905. Since then the New York Yankees have won the most World Series.

Most teenagers play baseball in high school for the love of the game, though some hope for a shot at the big leagues.

to-head with the NL in places such as Boston, Chicago, and Philadelphia. The AL also offered pay raises to NL stars and enticed many to "jump" to the new league. Fearing financial ruin, the NL declared a **truce**, and the leagues agreed to cooperate to ensure the success of professional baseball.

School Days

College baseball was introduced in the 1800s and high school baseball around the turn of the 20th century. College educators were fond of the game, but only as an amateur sport. Students who considered going pro were strongly discouraged from doing so. Often, graduates were offered a job (such as coaching the university's baseball team) to keep them on campus.

The college game continued to grow in the 20th century. In 1947, the first College World Series was held. Former president George H. W. Bush was on the Yale Univer-

12

sity squad that advanced to the finals. His career ended shortly thereafter, but that's not true of today's top collegiate players. They use their college experience to propel them to stardom in the majors.

High school players have also long dreamed of big-league careers. The very best suit up each spring hoping to be discovered by a professional scout. High school coaches, especially those on the varsity level, are often former players who were not nearly good enough for the majors, but still enjoy being involved in the game.

A Man Named Babe

For the first two decades of the 20th century, pitchers ruled the diamond. Mound heroes such as Christy Mathewson, Grover Cleveland Alexander, and Walter Johnson often squared off in tense, low-scoring battles. Fans came to love this brand of baseball. They turned out in such great numbers that most teams replaced their old, wooden ballparks with bigger stadiums made of concrete and steel.

The Polo Grounds, rebuilt in 1911 after a fire, was New York's first modern stadium.

With his mighty swing and larger-than-life personality, Babe Ruth ushered in an exciting new era of baseball.

In the years following World War I, the tastes of baseball fans suddenly changed. The crowds of the 1920s wanted to see a different game, one with lots of slugging and scoring. A livelier and cleaner ball provided a big boost in offense, but it was one man who hoisted the sport onto his shoulders and carried it into this exciting new era. His name was George Herman "Babe" Ruth, and he demolished almost every power hitting record in the books. Other players copied his style, and within

Here Comes the Judge

After a World Series betting scandal rocked baseball, major league owners hired a federal judge named Kenesaw Mountain Landis to be the game's first commissioner in 1920. Landis, always a friend to the owners, ruled with an iron fist for twenty-four years.

a few years home runs were flying out of ballparks at an astonishing rate. Ever since Ruth, the home run has been baseball's biggest weapon.

Breaking New Ground

For the first seventy-five years of professional baseball, two games were being played—one by Caucasians and one by people of color. Since the majors were not yet **integrated**, the only option for African-Americans and others was the Negro

Unfortunately, many of the Negro League All-Stars pictured here never got the chance to display their extraordinary talents in the majors.

Leagues. The top Negro League players were as good as the best major leaguers (they often met in post-season exhibitions), but organized baseball always found a way to keep them out. In the 1920s, **racism** against African-Americans was especially strong. During the 1930s, hard times brought on by the Great Depression kept baseball from opening its doors to Negro Leaguers.

In 1945, Branch Rickey, the general manager of the Brooklyn Dodgers, plotted to smash through baseball's color barrier. To pull off his plan, he needed to find a black player with the physical skills to excel on the field and the **resolve** to endure the hatred and racial slurs leveled at him. Rickey chose Jackie Robinson, a former Army officer and college man who had world-class skills in half a dozen sports. Robinson made it to the majors in 1947 and led the Dodgers to the World Series. He went on to have a Hall of Fame career, and proved forever that the color of a player's skin has nothing to do with his ability to play winning baseball.

After Robinson made his breakthrough, other teams began signing black and Latino players. In a span of just twenty years, a generation of exciting stars—including Henry Aaron, Willie Mays, Ernie Banks, Frank Robinson, Bob Gibson, Juan Marichal, and Roberto Clemente—had helped elevate the quality of play and enabled the major leagues to expand from sixteen teams to twenty-four. On the field and in the stands, baseball reflected America's growing cultural **diversity**.

Eyes of the Nation

The 1947 World Series was the first to be televised coast to coast.

Jackie Robinson, shown here stealing home in the 1955 World Series, broke baseball's color barrier in 1947.

Roberto Clemente, part of baseball's new wave of stars in the 1960s, could win a game with his bat and his glove.

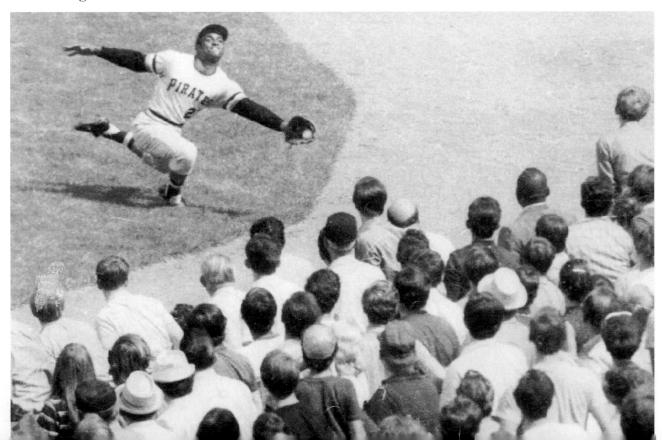

Girl Power

During World War II, many professional players were pressed into military service. With the level of play declining, Phil Wrigley, the owner of the Chicago Cubs, offered fans an alternative: women's professional softball. In 1943, he was convinced to go a step further and start the All-American Girls Professional Baseball League. The league lasted ten years. These baseball pioneers were immortalized in the 1992 movie *A League of Their Own*. Pictured above is Jean Marlowe, who played in the AAGPBL from 1948 to 1954.

Hard Labor

In 1970, an All-Star outfielder named Curt Flood sparked a series of events that transformed professional baseball. When the St. Louis Cardinals traded him to Philadelphia, he refused to go, and chose to challenge the 100-year-old reserve clause in court. Seven years later, players won the right to become free agents and auction their services to the highest bidder.

Although many people feared that baseball's new economic structure would ruin the sport, free agency at first seemed to help baseball. Attendance increased, and fans loved the fact that their teams could get a good player without having to trade a good player in return. But trouble began in the 1980s. Twice the players went on strike because of labor disagreements. The owners tried to control high salaries by secretly —and illegally—agreeing not to sign each other's free agents. When another work stoppage occurred in 1994 and the World Series was cancelled, many fans turned their back on America's pastime.

The players and owners won them back thanks to a power display that recalled the days of Babe Ruth—only this time it took two sluggers to do the trick. In 1998, Mark McGwire and Sammy Sosa staged a memorable battle to break the single-season homer record. The duel energized baseball, and helped

Mark McGwire's mammoth home runs helped baseball regain its popularity with fans.

19

Glamour Guys

Thanks to Babe Ruth, home run records are the most glamorous in all of sports. When the "Bambino" retired in 1935, he held the marks for most homers in a season (60) and in a career (714). Anyone who approached these records in the following years received tremendous publicity. Roger Maris caused an uproar when he broke the single-season mark in 1961. The same thing happened in 1974 when Henry Aaron (right) slammed his 715th home run. Since then Barry Bonds has thrilled fans with his pursuit of both records, including his record 73 home runs in 2001.

many fans rediscover their love of the sport. When McGwire established a new mark with 70 homers in one season, baseball's comeback was complete.

Today, more than 10 million men, women, and children play baseball in pick-up games and in organized leagues. They spend hundreds of millions of dollars on bats, gloves, base-balls, and other equipment. Meanwhile, despite some economic problems, professional baseball is still extremely popular. And going to the ballpark has never been more fun. Major league teams are building breathtaking new stadiums with everything from **retractable** roofs to swimming pools. Minor league baseball is booming, too. And as always, the face of the game reflects the changing cultural forces in the United States. A wave of stars has arrived from Asia and Latin America, bringing new sights, sounds, and flavors to the national pastime. Some say baseball has never been better. Others believe the best is yet to come.

Learning the fundamentals at a young age is key to becoming a good player.

Chapter Two

Play Ball!

If you've stood in the **batter's box** even once, you know how difficult it is to hit a baseball. Here's a secret: Major Leaguers understand how you feel. Professionals may make the game look easy, but don't be fooled. They were kids once, too, and had to learn the proper way to hit, field, and throw. The keys to improving as a ballplayer are first acquiring the skills needed on the field, then practicing them.

In the Field

In a regulation baseball game, nine players take the field. Six players, including the pitcher and catcher, are responsible

Viewed from above, it is easy to see why a baseball field is also known as a "diamond."

The Heat Is On

Third base is nicknamed the "hot corner." Why? Because third basemen often stand closer to home plate than the other infielders, and batted balls reach them in a flash.

for what happens on the infield. Viewing the diamond from home plate, the third baseman and shortstop stand on the left side of second base, while the first baseman and second baseman are on the right side. Positioned behind them are the left fielder, center fielder, and right fielder.

Playing the infield requires quick reflexes, sure hands, and accurate throws. The shortstop and third baseman normally have the strongest arms because their tosses to first base must travel all the way across the diamond. Many chances infielders get are on ground balls. What is proper technique for fielding a grounder? Eyes on the ball, glove on the ground, and body in front of the bouncer. Don't panic if the ball takes a bad hop. Try to knock it down, pick it up, and make a good throw to the correct base.

On hits to the outfield, infielders are responsible for setting up a relay. They position themselves in a line between the outfielder and where the ball needs to go. Communication is crucial. One infielder takes the throw from the outfield, while another yells where the ball goes next. If that infielder is not loud enough or another teammate is also screaming, the relay man might get confused.

The left fielder, center fielder, and right fielder are the last line of defense. If a ball gets by them, it's likely the batter will advance an extra base or two. That's why outfielders must talk with each other, especially on balls hit between them. If one thinks he can catch a long drive, he must yell "I got it!" or "Mine!" This tells the other outfielder to back him up just in case he misses the ball.

Tracking down fly balls requires speed, but it's not essential. Good outfielders concentrate on the batter. Watching the swing, they listen to the sound of bat against ball. A sharp crack off a wooden bat or high-pitched ping off an aluminum bat means the ball will travel far. A dull thud suggests the

Center Stage

The center fielder is in charge in the outfield. If he calls for a fly ball, the other fielders should get out of his way.

Outfielders avoid collisions on balls hit between them by calling out who should make the catch.

All-Star Vladimir Guerrero stretches high to snag a long drive.

Glove Work

Gloves first appeared around 1875, though many players didn't use them. The first models were actually fingerless palm pads. Today, outfielders like large gloves that help them snare drives over their heads. First basemen also use bigger gloves, because they sometimes must scoop bad throws in the dirt. Infielders prefer smaller gloves that make it easy to transfer the ball to their throwing hand. The catcher's mitt is rounded to give pitchers a good target.

opposite. The quicker an outfielder can read the flight of the ball, the better his chance of catching it.

Outfielders often need to make throws back to the infield or all the way to home plate. Because of the relay, accuracy is just as important as arm strength. A quick, hard throw to the cutoff is always better than a long heave that sails wide or high over its target.

Pitch and Catch

Pitcher and catcher are the game's most specialized positions. The relationship between these two is crucial. When a hurler and his backstop aren't in sync, the scoreboard usually lights up with runs.

There is more to pitching than trying to burn a fastball past a hitter. The goal is to prevent the batter from making solid contact with the ball. Sometimes a hard one right down the middle is the best choice. But if the hitter is expecting a fastball, a slower pitch thrown inside, outside, high, or low is more effective. The point is that precision and **finesse** are as critical as pure power.

A pitcher's best friend is the catcher. A backstop's first job is to help decide what pitch to throw. Since catchers squat behind the plate, they are in perfect position to learn the weaknesses of hitters. The catcher is also the captain of the infield. For example, he lets his teammates know how to shift if a **sacrifice bunt** is attempted.

The wear and tear on catchers can take its toll. They have to block wild pitches in the dirt, be ready to fire quick throws to nab base runners, and think constantly about opposing hitters. Most backstops put up with the pain and pressure because they love the responsibility that comes with their position.

All-Star catcher Ivan "Pudge" Rodriguez dives to catch a foul pop-up.

Good hitters never take their eyes off the ball.

Batter Up

What are the keys to hitting? Watch the ball from the moment it leaves the pitcher's hand, and follow it all the way to home plate. Also, try to stay balanced. A good swing incorporates the entire body, not just the arms. Power comes from a smooth turn of the legs and hips toward the ball. Quick wrists and hands are the key to whipping the bat through the strike zone.

Of course, players in amateur leagues enjoy the extra power supplied by aluminum bats. By contrast, these specially designed, lightweight models are not allowed in the big leagues. Professionals at all levels are required to use wooden bats.

Obviously, every team has different types of hitters. That's the challenge managers face when making a lineup. The ideal batting order capitalizes on each player's strengths. Usually, hitters who get on base and run well occupy the top two spots. The next four are reserved for batters with power who drive in runs. The final three hitters differ from lineup to lineup.

Head Gear

Players started experimenting with versions of the batting helmet in 1907. Big leaguers weren't required to wear them until fifty years later. Today everyone must use a helmet. Youth models have two earflaps, and some include a facemask.

Whether at the plate or in the field, good baseball teams work together. In the dugout, players discuss the opposing pitcher's strengths and weaknesses. When a batter makes an out, teammates find out why and learn from it. On defense, every fielder has a responsibility on every play, from chasing down a hit to covering a base to backing up a teammate. And everyone, whether a starter or reserve, should support his teammates enthusiastically.

The dugout is a great place to talk strategy— and make friends.

Not everyone agrees with the decisions made by umpires, but no one knows the rules better than the "men in blue."

Chapter Three

Check the Rule Book

Who has the most difficult job in base-ball? It might be the umpires. Umps have to make split-second decisions, at times under extreme pressure. If they miss a call, fans—and sometimes players and managers—scream in protest. How do good umpires deal with the strain? By learning all the rules. But that's not easy. The official rule book is more than a hundred pages long.

Players can try to catch fly balls and pop-ups that drift into the stands, although they sometimes have to battle fans to make the play.

The Basics

Anyone who has played or watched baseball knows that the object is to score more runs than the opponent. Major League games last nine innings, unless they go into **extra innings**. Youth leagues play fewer innings. The home team always hits in the bottom half of each inning.

On all baseball fields, the bases are placed in the shape of a square, with the pitcher's rubber located in the middle. Fair territory is determined by the foul lines that run from home plate through the outside edge of first base and third base. Some fields, including those in the majors, have a fence that encloses the outfield. Any fair ball that clears this wall on a fly is a home run. Players are allowed to reach over the fence to catch a pop fly.

Any ground ball that crosses inside or over first base or third base is fair, even if it bounces into foul territory afterward. Fly balls and line drives to the outfield are fair if they fall inside a foul line or on it. A long drive that bangs off one of the foul poles down the right field or left field line is a home run.

Each team gets three outs per inning. Three strikes is an out. Four balls is a walk. Any fly ball or line drive caught in the air is an out. On grounders, an out is recorded when a fielder stops the ball and throws to first base before the batter reaches it. (Of course, the first baseman has to keep his foot on the base when catching the throw.) Force outs come into play whenever a runner occupies first, runners are on first and second, or the bases are loaded. In these situations, a fielder who scoops up a

Derek Jeter of the New York Yankees drops to one knee to backhand a groundball.

Men in Blue

Originally, the job of umpire was a great honor. Before each game, a volunteer was picked from the crowd or from one of the competing teams. The lucky winner worked alone, kneeling along the first base line. It wasn't until 1878 that umps were paid. Several years later, they began wearing blue caps and jackets. (In fact, umps are all still nicknamed "Blue.") In 1887, groups of umpires began calling games. In the majors today, four are assigned to each game, unless it's the playoffs, when six work together.

grounder can flip the ball to any base to which a runner is advancing. The runner is out if the toss beats him to the base. In addition, any runner not on a base can be tagged out with the ball.

Close Calls

Some rules are trickier than others. For example, what is the strike zone? According to the rule book, it is an imaginary box above home plate that starts just below the hitter's knees and goes to the midpoint between the top of his shoulders and the top of his uniform pants. Any pitch that crosses through this area is a strike. The problem is that every umpire has a different perspective. Some call strikes exactly as the rule states. Others **deviate** slightly, perhaps widening or lowering the strike zone.

How does a batter strike out? There are three ways to notch the third strike: A hitter can swing and miss, tip a pitch into the catcher's glove, or get caught looking at a pitch called strike three by the ump.

What about running the bases? A runner can only advance to the next base if a teammate doesn't occupy it. Passing a base runner is an automatic out. When fly balls or line drives are snagged in the air, every runner has to go back to his base. A base runner can be thrown out if the defense gets the ball to his base before he returns.

In some leagues stealing is allowed. This means a runner can take off for the next base as the pitcher makes his delivery

Opposite: If a batter swings at a pitch— even if it does not cross home plate—it is ruled a strike.

Sliding into a base is one way to avoid being tagged out by a fielder with the ball.

to the plate. But stealing a base isn't as easy as it seems. Good catchers can make perfect throws to any base in a flash, and infielders with fast hands can apply quick tags. Pitchers also shorten their wind-ups and go from the stretch to keep runners from taking big leads. The "balk" rule, however, prohibits hurlers from **deceiving** base runners. For example, once a pitcher is on the rubber, he can't pretend to throw home and then toss the ball to a base.

Another way to advance on the bases is tagging up. On any fly ball, a runner can retreat to his base and then race toward the next one as soon as the pop-up is caught. He is safe if he arrives there before being tagged.

Swing Time

The rules affecting pitching have changed more than any others, especially in the majors. In the 1800s, before calling a ball, umpires issued warnings for the first couple **wayward** deliveries. A batter hit by a pitch wasn't awarded first base. Pitchers could stop their windup at any moment to catch **unsuspecting** runners off base.

By the 1900s, pitchers were moved back to the distance of 60 feet, 6 inches (18m, 15 cm). The pitcher's mound was introduced. So was the pitching rubber, and hurlers were required to keep contact with it until releasing the ball. Trick pitches like spitballs were banned. Foul balls were counted as strikes for the first time.

Pitching in the big leagues today is extremely challenging. That's because there is so much emphasis on scoring. The ball has been slightly modified, and home runs have increased. The league has also instructed umpires to pay more attention to the rule book when calling strikes. This means that pitches just a bit inside or outside are now often called balls.

Over and Out

There are two instances when a player can **overrun** a base with worrying about being tagged out. The first is when a hitter sprints from the batter's box in hopes of beating a throw to first base. The second is when a runner crosses home plate.

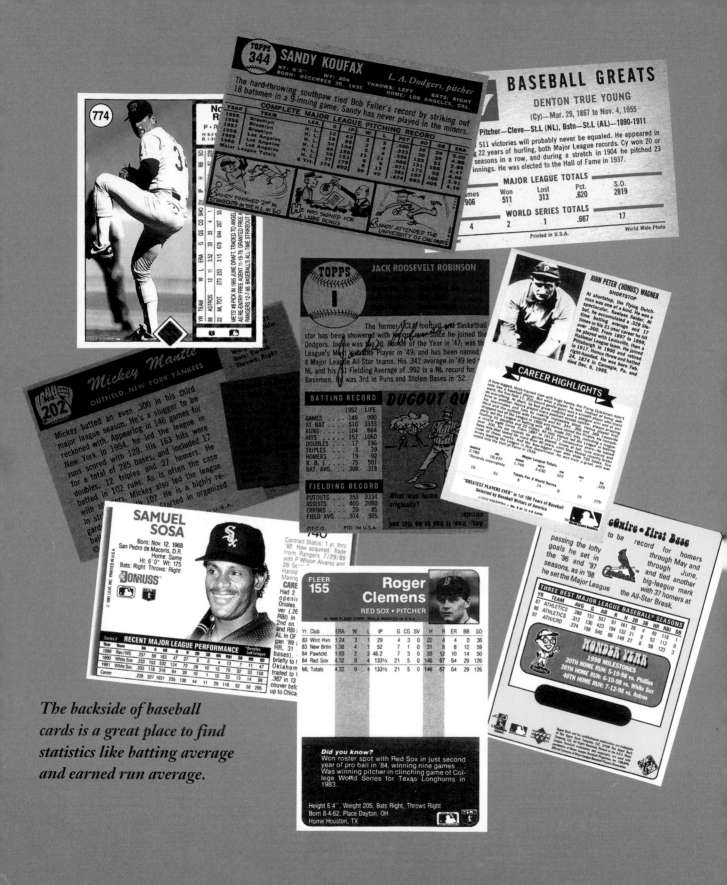

The backside of baseball cards is a great place to find statistics like batting average and earned run average.

Chapter Four

Numbers Game

Did your favorite player have a good rookie season? Check his statistics. A big leaguer with a batting average (AVG. or BA) above .300 is considered an excellent hitter. A pitcher with an earned run average (ERA) less than 3.00 is tough to beat. Stats are important because they serve as permanent records of baseball history. Utilizing them to evaluate a player is just one of their many uses.

Statistically Speaking

Baseball stats have been kept since the 1850s. Back then supporters of baseball wanted to **distinguish** the sport from other games and offer it a higher measure of respect. Given America's growing fascination with science and technology, they decided to chart the performance of players. There were twenty-three official offensive, defensive, and pitching statistics in the 19th century. Today that number has more than doubled.

The primary offensive stats are AVG., runs (R), hits (H), doubles (2B), triples (3B), home runs (HR), runs batted in (RBI), walks (BB), strikeouts (SO), on-base average (OBA), and stolen bases (SB). Pitching stats include wins (W), losses (L), saves (S), innings pitched (IP), hits allowed (H), walks, strikeouts (K), and ERA. The fielding stats referenced most often are putouts (PO), assists (A), errors (E) and fielding average (FA).

Some of these require explanation. RBIs describe how many baserunners a batter drives home. (Remember that a solo home run is worth one RBI.) OBA indicates how often a batter reaches base via hit, walk, or hit-by-pitch (HBP). Earned runs are runs charged to a pitcher that aren't the result

Read All About It!

The first baseball **box score** appeared in the *New York Morning News* in 1845.

Keeping Score

The "father" of baseball statistics is a reporter named Henry Chadwick. In the 1850s he devised a scorekeeping method that made it easy to tally each player's statistics. His system is still used today.

Before he joined the Seattle Mariners in 2001, Ichiro Suzuki was the best hitter in Japan.

Book Report

The first book to offer career statistics on big leaguers was *Who's Who in Baseball*, published in 1912.

of an error. ERA reveals how many earned runs a pitcher surrenders every nine innings. Putouts are recorded when a fielder snags a flyball, tags a runner, or receives a throw for a force-out. (Catchers are also credited with a putout when they catch a third strike.) Assists are registered when a fielder makes a throw that leads to an out.

Do the Math

Want to know something surprising? Baseball statistics are a great way to learn math. That's because many stats are derived from basic arithmetic.

Lots of statistics are represented by decimals, which are calculated with long division. For example, batting average divides a player's hits by his at-bats (not including walks, HBPs, and sacrifices). On the other hand, a stat known as "total bases" is computed with multiplication and addition. Singles are multiplied by 1, doubles by 2, triples by 3, and home runs by 4. When these four numbers are added together, they equal the total number of bases a player has **amassed**.

Behind the Numbers

Which statistics are most significant? The ones tied most closely to winning and losing. For example, offensive stats such as runs and RBIs are important because they show how many runs a player produces for his team. Batting average is a good indicator of a player's individual success. But batting average with runners in scoring position (that is, on second or third base) says more about his value to his team.

Card Game

The back of a baseball card is a great place to find stats. Trading cards first hit the scene in the 1860s. Candy and bubble gum makers began including them in packages forty years later. It wasn't until the 1950s that statistics started to appear on baseball cards.

For pitchers, wins are the first stat experts examine. ERA is meaningful, too. A low ERA usually suggests a hurler has pitched well, even if his team has a losing record. Another interesting mound stat is ratio. This measures the number of base runners a pitcher allows every nine innings. The lower the number, the less trouble a pitcher faces.

Today, baseball statistics are used in a variety of ways. Millions of fans participate in fantasy leagues, which challenge competitors to assemble their own teams of big leaguers. The better numbers their players put up, the better their team does. Agents rely heavily on statistics when **negotiating** new contracts for players. Stats also play a role in determining who makes it into the Baseball Hall of Fame. Voters refer to all sorts of numbers to figure out which players are worthy of induction. But they remember that statistics don't always tell the whole story. Nothing beats seeing a player in person.

Troy Percival had 40 saves and a 1.92 ERA in 2002, and helped the Anaheim Angels win the World Series.

Babe Ruth, considered by many to be baseball's all-time best hitter, started his career as a pitcher.

Chapter Five

The Great Debate

Who's the greatest hitter ever? Who's the top pitcher? Fans have argued these questions for as long as baseball has been played. That's one of the fun things about the sport. Everyone has an opinion about baseball's best. To help you hold your own in any debate, here's a look at some of the game's most notable players. The first group consists of old-timers who played before World War II. The second lists those who have played in the last sixty years.

Timeless Classics

In the eyes of many fans, no one will ever surpass Babe Ruth. The "Sultan of Swat" ranks second all-time in home runs and runs batted in. His batting average is among the ten best in history. But Ruth was more than a slugger. His New York Yankees won the World Series five times in the 1920s and 1930s. He also notched 80 wins as a pitcher before he became an everyday outfielder in 1919 for the Yanks.

Ty Cobb finished his career with the highest batting average (.366) in baseball history. But what set the "Georgia Peach" apart was a fierce desire to win. It also made him the most hated man in the sport. Honus Wagner, a barrel-chested shortstop who played in the early 1900s, was beloved by players and fans alike. Wagner's versatility was legendary. The "Flying Dutchman" could play any infield position, batted for average and power, and was a master thief on the bases.

Napoleon Lajoie was another hard-hitting infielder. A graceful second baseman, he batted .426 in 1901, still the

Gold Standard

Gold Gloves are awarded each year to the top fielders in each league. They were presented for the first time in 1958.

Cap and King

In the 19th century, Adrian "Cap" Anson and Mike "King" Kelly were baseball's biggest stars. During his 27-season career, Anson batted higher than .380 three times. He was also a great manager. Anson was a tremendous **strategist** whose innovations included the hit-and-run, the use of a pitching rotation, and the introduction of spring training.

Kelly starred on five of Anson's championship teams. The cleverest player of his time, he looked like a movie star and lived like one. He earned his nickname both for his sterling play on the field and his royal lifestyle off it.

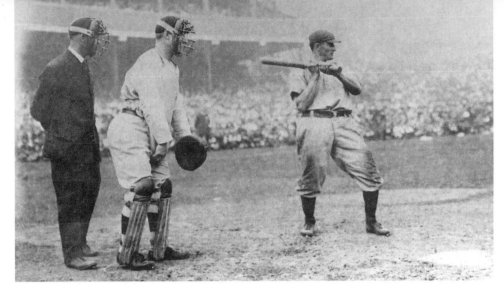

Honus Wagner (holding the bat) was the National League's top shortstop for two decades in the early 1900s.

American League record. Joe Jackson might have beaten Lajoie's mark, had he not been banned from baseball for his participation in the plot to throw the 1919 World Series. "Shoeless" Joe has the third highest career average (.356) of all time. His swing was so sweet that even Ruth tried to copy it.

Denton "Cy" Young uncovered the secret to pitching **longevity**: proper mechanics and physical fitness. From 1890 to 1911, he won 511 games. Today, the Cy Young Award is given annually to the top hurler in each

Cy Young recorded more than 500 wins during his amazing career.

The Yankee Clipper

No one cut a more **dignified** figure than Joe DiMaggio. The "Yankee Clipper" never gave less than his all, yet he did everything on the field with effortless grace. DiMaggio led New York to nine world titles. He recorded a record 56-game hitting streak in 1941.

league. Christy Mathewson was a genius on the mound who confounded hitters with his fade-away pitch. The ultimate control artist, he threw three shutouts in six days for the New York Giants in the 1905 World Series. Robert "Lefty" Grove showed pitchers how to adapt to change. As a rookie in 1925, he had a scorching fastball that few batters could hit. By the end of his career, with his arm worn down, Grove featured a masterful array of curves and off-speed pitches. He retired with 300 wins and 55 saves.

Modern Marvels

No one has ever analyzed or understood hitting as well as Ted Williams. If the "Splendid Splinter" didn't swing at a pitch, umpires were hesitant to call it a strike. For his career he hit .344 with 521 home runs. Just as impressive was his .482 on-base average.

Henry Aaron, Willie Mays, and Mickey Mantle rose to prominence in the 1950s, but their all-around talents would

On the Outside

Neither Josh Gibson nor Leroy "Satchel" Paige spent a day in the majors during their primes because of baseball's color barrier. In fact Gibson never made it there at all. A talented catcher, he slugged some of the longest home runs anyone has ever seen. Paige, blessed with an indestructible right arm, started his career in 1926 in the Negro Leagues. Twenty-two years later, he helped the Cleveland Indians win the pennant. In 1965, at nearly sixty years old, he pitched three scoreless innings for the Kansas City Athletics.

Mickey Mantle, the greatest switch-hitter ever, was dangerous from both sides of the plate.

have made them stars in any era. "Hammerin' Hank" is baseball's all-time home run king with 755 long balls. Mantle, who won the Triple Crown in 1956, possessed an explosive combination of speed and power. Mays, known as the "Say Hey Kid," was the most exciting player ever to step on the diamond. This trio of do-it-all stars stood out during a time when baseball was beginning to turn to specialists like relievers, defensive replacements, and platoon players.

Jackie Robinson will always be remembered for the courage he displayed as the majors' first black player. But some fans forget the other ways he reshaped the game. With his speed and daring, Robinson showed how to win with his legs, glove, and mind.

Fans adored catcher Yogi Berra because he looked and talked like a fan watching a game, not a star playing in one. On the field, however, he was one of history's great clutch

Big Three

Triple Crown is a term used when a player leads his league in batting average, home runs, and RBIs.

A Real Whiz

Though he batted only .262 for his career, shortstop Ozzie Smith was an easy choice for the Hall of Fame. Why? Because the "Wizard of Oz" was a breathtaking infielder whose sure hands and acrobatic flair set the standard for defense at his position.

performers. Berra was the heart and soul of ten Yankee champions during the 1940s, 1950s, and 1960s. Johnny Bench was the main cog in Cincinnati's "Big Red Machine" of the 1970s. The two-time MVP **revolutionized** his position by catching pitches with one hand. This style helped him avoid injury and made it easier to throw out base stealers.

Sandy Koufax combined an explosive fastball and a sharp-breaking curve. It took the left-hander many years to control these pitches, but once he did he was unhittable. From 1963 to 1966, he won 97 games and struck out 1,228 batters. Nolan Ryan redefined the term power pitcher. Though his career spanned four decades, his fastball never lost its sizzle. He holds the record for strikeouts (5,714) and no-hitters (7).

Of today's players, who will be added to the list of all-time greats? Certainly Randy Johnson and Roger Clemens qualify. They are modern versions of Koufax and Ryan. Mark McGwire and Barry Bonds belong there, too. So does Sammy Sosa, who in many ways symbolizes the true power and beauty of the sport. From a childhood of desperate hunger and poverty, he became the most recognized baseball player on the planet. Sosa found baseball, then baseball found him.

Where's the Fire?

Closers are a recent **phenomenon** in baseball. Who blazed the trail for them? Bruce Sutter. During his twelve-year career, he posted 300 saves with a darting, dipping split-fingered fastball.

Somewhere out there is the next Sammy Sosa. He may be a fifth grader cracking a homer in a Little League game across town, or an eight-year-old scooping up grounders on a pebble-strewn infield in a country you've never heard of. Or maybe, just maybe, that kid is you.

Baseball used to be a pastime only in America. Now kids all over the world play the game.

Hot Stuff

Who has handled the heat best at the hot corner? Brooks Robinson was the top fielder, and Mike Schmidt was the most devastating hitter. Right behind this pair were Eddie Mathews and George Brett.

Timeline

1846	The first official baseball game; the New York Knickerbockers lose 23-1 to the New York Club.
1849	The Knickerbockers introduce baseball's first uniforms.
1857	Games are changed to nine innings, instead of the format that declared the winner as the first team to score 21 runs.
1876	The National League is formed.
1879	The National League introduces the reserve clause.
1884	Pitchers are allowed to throw overhand.
1889	Baseball decides on three strikes and four balls.
1897	Cap Anson becomes the first player to reach 3,000 hits.
1903	The first World Series of the modern era is played.
1908	The first electronic scoreboard is introduced.
1910	William Taft becomes the first president to throw out the first ball on Opening Day.
1917	America enters World War I, and baseball stadiums begin playing the "Star Spangled Banner" before games.
1921	A Major League game is broadcast on radio for the first time.
1927	Babe Ruth sets a new record with 60 home runs in one season.
1933	The first All-Star Game is played.
1935	The majors play the first night game.

1936	The Hall of Fame is established.
1939	A baseball game is televised for the first time.
1941	Joe DiMaggio hits in fifty-six games in a row.
1947	Jackie Robinson breaks baseball's color barrier.
1954	The Negro American League plays its final season.
1961	Roger Maris hits 61 home runs to break Babe Ruth's single-season record.
1969	The majors expand to twenty-four teams with the addition of the San Diego Padres, Montreal Expos, Kansas City Royals, and Seattle Pilots.
1970	Curt Flood sues Major League Baseball.
1973	The American League adopts the designated hitter rule.
1974	Henry Aaron surpasses Babe Ruth as baseball's all-time home run king.
1985	Pete Rose breaks Ty Cobb's record for career hits.
1992	The Toronto Blue Jays become the first team outside the U.S. to win the World Series.
1998	Mark McGwire sets a new single-season home run record with 70.
2001	Barry Bonds breaks McGwire's record with 73 homers.
2003	Sammy Sosa becomes the first Latino to hit 500 home runs in the majors.

Glossary

amass—to collect or accumulate things

batter's box—rectangular boxes on each side of home plate inside which batters must stand when hitting

box score—a statistical rundown of a baseball game

deceive—to intentionally fool someone into believing something that isn't true

deviate—to be different or stray from how something is normally done

dignified—to show self-respect and behave in a proper way

distinguish—to set something apart from something else

diversity—a variety of something, including ethnic background

extra innings—innings added to the end of a baseball game that isn't decided in regulation. Teams play one extra inning at a time until one of them wins.

finesse—delicate and skillful

integrated—open to everyone without restrictions on things such as race or ethnicity

longevity—a long duration of time

negotiate—to talk things over until an agreement is reached

overrun—in baseball, to run past a base

pastime—an interest or activity that somebody pursues in his or her spare time

phenomenon—an occurrence that is out of the ordinary

racism—prejudice against a group of people because of their race

raucous—loud and rowdy

resolve—staying true to a belief or course of action

retractable—something that can be opened and closed

revolutionize—to cause a radical change in something

ruthless—having no mercy

sacrifice bunt—a play in baseball when a batter bunts the ball to advance runners on base

shrewd—inclined to deal with matters in a clever and intelligent way

strategist—someone who plans ahead and thinks well on his feet

truce—an agreed break that ends a fight or disagreement

unsuspecting—unaware of what's going to happen next

wayward—wild and unpredictable

To Find Out More

Books

Egan, Terry; Friedman, Stan, and Levine, Mike. *MacMillan Book of Baseball Stories*. New York, NY: MacMillan Publishing Company, 1992.

Gutman, Dan. *The Way Baseball Works*. New York, NY: Simon & Schuster, 1996

Kelley, James. *Eyewitness Baseball*. New York, NY: Dorling Kindersley, 2000.

Ritter, Lawrence. *The Story of Baseball*. New York, NY: William Morrow and Company, 1983.

Stewart, Mark. *Baseball: A History of the National Pastime*. Danbury, CT: Franklin Watts, 1998.

Stewart, Mark. *The World Series*. Danbury, CT: Franklin Watts, 2002.

Any of the baseball biographies in the New Wave series by Mark Stewart published by the Millbrook Press.

Organizations and Online Sites

http://www.ballparks.com
An interesting site devoted to baseball stadiums, past and present.

http://negroleaguebaseball.com
Learn about the history of the Negro Leagues, including information on great teams and players.

Little League Baseball
http://www.littleleague.org
Official site of Little League Baseball. Learn about the history of Little League and where to find leagues in your area.

Major League Baseball

http://www.mlb.com

Official site of Major League Baseball. Get news, stats, scores, and anything else you need to know about your favorite teams and players.

Minor League Baseball

http://www.minorleaguebaseball.com

Official site of Minor League Baseball. Get the latest information on every minor league team.

National Amateur Baseball Federation

http://nabf.com

Official site of the NABF. Learn about the history of America's oldest amateur baseball association and how to join a league in your area.

National Baseball Hall of Fame and Museum

http://www.baseballhalloffame.org

Official site of the Baseball Hall of Fame. Find out about honorees, exhibits, and visitor information.

USA Baseball

http://www.usabaseball.com

Official site of USA Baseball. Keep up-to-date with every national baseball team that represents the United States, including the Olympic team.

A Note on Sources

In researching this book, I tried to reference as many sources as possible. I consulted another author named Mark Stewart, who has written books on baseball, including biographies of famous players. I also read other insightful books, such as *Total Baseball* and *The All Century Team*. Web sites on the Internet, including the one hosted by Major League Baseball, were helpful as well.

In addition, I drew on my personal knowledge of baseball. I played in college and in organized leagues after graduation, and have coached for many years in Little League and high school. These experiences have taught me a great deal about the sport.

—*Mike Kennedy*

Index

Numbers in *italics* indicate illustrations.

About the Author

From Ichiro to the Indy 500 and the Super Bowl to skateboarding, Mike Kennedy has covered it all in the world of sports. A graduate of Franklin & Marshall College, he has profiled athletes such as Sammy Sosa, Tony Hawk, and Venus and Serena Williams. Mike has contributed his expertise to other books by Grolier/Scholastic, including *The World Series*, *The Super Bowl*, and *The NBA Finals*. He is also a co-creator of JockBio.com (*www.jockbio.com*), a unique website that profiles popular sports personalities.

His other titles in this series are *Basketball*, *Football*, *Ice Hockey*, *Roller Hockey*, *Skateboarding*, and *Soccer*.